BAGS OF POEMS

FAMILY ALBUM

Poems selected by Jill Bennett

Illustrated by Sami Sweeten

PICTURE CORGI BOOKS

Our Family Comes From Round the World

Our family comes
From round the world:
Our hair is straight,
Our hair is curled,
Our eyes are brown,
Our eyes are blue,
Our skins are different
Colours, too.

Tra la tra la
Tra la tra lee
We're one big happy family!

We're girls and boys,
We're big and small,
We're young and old,
We're short and tall.
We're everything
That we can be
And still we are
A family.

O la dee da
O la dee dee
We're one big happy family!

We laugh and cry,
We work and play,
We help each other
Every day.
The world's a lovely
Place to be
Because we are
A family.

Hurray hurrah
Hurrah hurree
We're one big happy family!

Mary Ann Hoberman

Ask Mummy Ask Daddy

When I ask Daddy
Daddy says ask Mummy

When I ask Mummy
Mummy says ask Daddy.
I don't know where to go.

Better ask my teddy
he never says no.

John Agard

The Irreplaceable Mum

If you were a crack in the mirror,
If you were a flea on a cat,
If you were a slug in a jug,
I'd still love you, I wouldn't mind that.

If you were a smudge on a picture
Or an opera singer struck dumb,
If you were a pain in the neck then
You'd still be my very best chum.

If you were a fly in a pizza,
If you were a difficult sum,
Even if you were humpy and grumpy
You'd still be irreplaceable, Mum.

Brian Patten

My Dad Calls Me

When I tell fibs
my dad calls me
Louis Lou Liar.

When I come in from playing
with my clothes a bit mucked up
he calls me
Dopey Dog Dirt.

When we were in this café
on holiday
and I laughed
and coughed orange juice all over the floor
my dad called me
Garry Gobhound.

When I watch telly
all Saturday morning and I get a bit dozy
my dad calls me
Wally Tellybrains.

When my nose is a bit runny
and I can't find my hanky
my dad calls me
King of the Bogies.

I call him
Nag Bag.

Michael Rosen

My Father

My father is tall
and strong as a giant.
I bet
with his bare hands
he could break rocks in half.
But when I told him this one day,
he picked me up
and held me close
so that I *felt* his tenderness and
the rumble of his laugh.

Charlotte Zolotow

New Baby

I like the magic number 3
the way it used to be,
when 1 was Mum
& 2 was Dad
& 3 was only me.

But 1 is growing fat and round
2 tiptoes past the door
& 3 is me
& counting
to the magic
number 4.

J. Patrick Lewis

My Baby Brother

My baby brother's beautiful,
So perfect and so tiny.
His skin is soft and velvet brown;
His eyes are dark and shiny.

His hair is black and curled up tight;
His two new teeth are sharp and white.
I like it when he chews his toes;
And when he laughs, his dimple shows.

Mary Ann Hoberman

My Baby Brother

My baby brother is so small,
he hasn't even learned to crawl.
He's only been around a week,
and all he seems to do is bawl
and wiggle, sleep . . . and leak.

Jack Prelutsky

My Little Sister

My sister
and I
always
fight.

I'm sure she's
wrong. I
think I'm
right.

She pinches my
toys
when I'm not
there

she cheats at
games.
She's never
fair.

She leaves her
clothes
all over the
place

if I complain
she pulls a
face.

Every
morning
I have to
wait

to take her
to school . . .
we're always
late . . .

but however
naughty
she can
be

nothing
must hurt her.
She's smaller
than me.

Ann Bonner

Mean Maxine

There's no one mean as mean Maxine,
she smells like old cigars,
her brain is smaller than a bean,
I wish she'd move to Mars.

Some day I'll list the things I hate,
and that is where I'll list her,
I'd like to pack her in a crate –
too bad Maxine's my sister.

Jack Prelutsky

Friends Again

My brother bashed me with a stick.
I hit him with the hose.
He pulled my hair. I scratched his face.
He thumped me on the nose.

I bit his leg; he screamed. *I* screamed.
We called each other names.
Then Mum came out and asked us why
We couldn't play nice games.

I sulked. He moped. I frowned. He smiled.
I let him in my den.
He offered me a sticky sweet,
And now we're friends again.

Paul Rogers

Granny

It so nice to have a Granny
when you've had it from yuh Mammy
and you feeling down and dammy

It so nice to have a Granny
when she brings you bread and jammy
and says, 'Tell it all to Granny.'

Grace Nichols

My Grannies

I hate it, in the holiday,
When Grandma brings her pets to stay –
Her goat, her pig, her seven rats
Scare our dog and chase our cats.
Her budgies bite, her parrots shout –
And guess who has to clean them out?

My other Gran, the one I like,
Always brings her motor-bike,
And when she takes me for a ride
To picnic in the countryside,
We zoom up hills and whizz round bends –
I hate it when her visit ends!

June Crebbin

Grandpa Never Sleeps

Grandpa doesn't sleep at night,
He never sleeps a wink.
Instead he tinkers with the car
Or mends the kitchen sink.

Sometimes he picks the rhubarb
Or polishes the floor.
And other nights he's shopping
At the local all-night store.

Last night he papered half the hall
And built a garden shed.
But when the rest of us got up
He *didn't* go to bed.

I don't know how he does it,
He's always on the go.
Grandpa never sleeps AT ALL –
At least, I think that's so . . .

Mark Burgess

Aunt Samantha

Aunt Samantha woke one day
and sat up in her bed,
when a middle-sized rhinoceros
sat squarely on her head.

She did not seem the least put out,
was not at all annoyed;
in fact, as she addressed the beast,
she sounded overjoyed.

'I'm very glad you're up there,
though you've squashed my head quite flat,
for you've saved me all the botherment
of putting on my hat.'

Jack Prelutsky

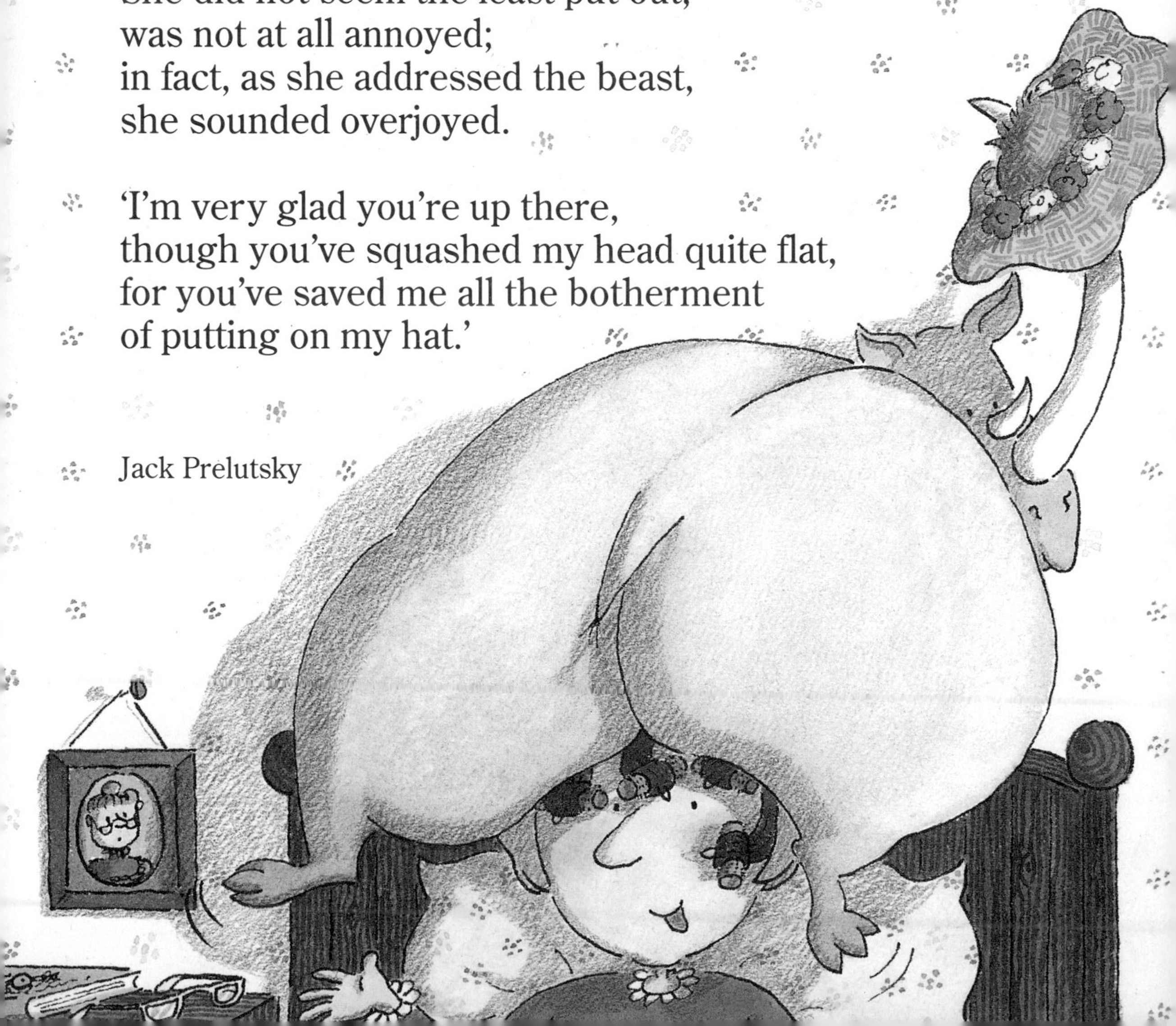

My Uncle's Umbrella
Under my uncle's umbrella
Are Uncle Augustus and I.
My uncle's quite fat –
If it wasn't for that,
I'd manage to keep myself dry.
Colin West

Cousins

Every evening
when the dark creeps in
like a smothering black cape,
our little family
– Mum, Dad, Brother, Sister, Gogo the Cat and me –
we get together to huddle and cuddle
and keep us each safe.

Every night
when the moon rises like a white saucer,
our little family
– Mum, Dad, Brother, Sister, Gogo the Cat and me –
go to bed in our warm rooms.
We tuck each other in
and sleep safe in green dreams.

But in another land
when the same dark creeps in,
a broken family in a wild wind
looks to the same moon, red and angry,
and each makes a wish.
– Mum, Dad, Brother, Sister, Asmara the Stray Dog –
all ask for food, for medicine, for peace, for rain.
Just these, only these, do our beautiful cousins ask for.

John Rice

for Vikram – JB
for Mum and Dad – SS

Thanks are due to the copyright holders for permission to include the following material in this collection:

John Agard, 'Ask Mummy Ask Daddy' from *I Din' Do Nuttin'*, published by The Bodley Head. © 1983 by John Agard. Ann Bonner, 'My Little Sister' from *You Just Can't Win* edited by Brian Moses and published by Blackie. © 1991 by Ann Bonner. Mark Burgess, 'Grandpa Never Sleeps' from *Can't Get to Sleep*, published by Methuen. © 1990 by Mark Burgess. June Crebbin, 'My Grannies' from *The Jungle Sale,* published by Viking. © 1988 by June Crebbin. Mary Ann Hoberman, 'Our Family Comes From Round the World' and 'My Baby Brother' from *Fathers, Mothers, Sisters, Brothers*, published by Little Brown Publishers Inc. © 1991 by Mary Ann Hoberman. J Patrick Lewis, 'New Baby'. © 1993 by J Patrick Lewis. Grace Nichols, 'Granny' from *No Hickory, No Dickory, No Dock*, published by Viking. © 1991 by Grace Nichols. Brian Patten, 'The Irreplaceable Mum' from *Thawing Frozen Frogs,* published by Viking. © 1990 by Brian Patten, reproduced with permission of Rogers, Coleridge and White Ltd. Jack Prelutsky, 'My Baby Brother' and 'Mean Maxine' from *A New Kid on the Block*, published by William Heinemann Ltd. © 1984 by Jack Prelutsky. And for 'Aunt Samantha' from *The Queen Eene*, published by Greenwillow Press. © 1970 by Jack Prelutsky. Paul Rogers, 'Friends Again'. © 1990 by Paul Rogers. John Rice, 'Cousins' from *Infant Projects: Families*, published by Scholastic. © 1971 by John Rice. Michael Rosen, 'My Dad Calls Me' from *The Hypnotiser*, published by Andre Deutsch Ltd. © 1988 by Michael Rosen. Colin West, 'My Uncle's Umbrella' from *What would you do with a Wobble-dee-Woo?*, published by Hutchinson Ltd. © 1988 by Colin West. Charlotte Zolotow, 'My Father' from *Everything Glistens and Everything Sings*, published by Harcourt Brace Jovanovich Inc. © 1987 by Charlotte Zolotow. Every effort has been made to trace and contact copyright holders before publication. If any errors or omissions occur the publisher will be pleased to rectify these at the earliest opportunity.

BAGS OF POEMS: FAMILY ALBUM
A PICTURE CORGI BOOK : 0 552 52715 7

First published in Great Britain by Doubleday,
a division of Transworld Publishers Ltd

PRINTING HISTORY
Doubleday edition published 1993
Picture Corgi edition published 1995

Picture Corgi Books are published by
Transworld Publishers Ltd,
61–63 Uxbridge Road, Ealing, London W5 5SA,
in Australia by Transworld Publishers (Australia) Pty. Ltd,
15–25 Helles Avenue, Moorebank, NSW 2170,
and in New Zealand by Transworld Publishers (NZ) Ltd,
3 William Pickering Drive, Albany, Auckland.

Printed and bound in Portugal by Printer Portuguesa